With Wings As Eagles

With Wings As Eagles

Andrew Murray

Whitaker House

All Scripture quotations are from the *King James Version* (KJV) of the Bible.

WITH WINGS AS EAGLES

ISBN: 0-88368-262-1
Printed in the United States of America
Copyright © 1996 by Whitaker House

Whitaker House
580 Pittsburgh Street
Springdale, PA 15144

3 4 5 6 7 8 9 10 11 12 / 06 05 04 03 02 01 00 99 98 97 96

Preface

This little volume passes on to its readers the words spoken by Andrew Murray at the meetings for United Prayer held in Exeter Hall on Thursday, December 5, 1895. It was a memorable day and brought to a close the labors of Mr. Murray's memorable visit to this country. On Saturday, December 7, Mr. and Mrs. Murray started on their return voyage to the Cape.

Mr. Murray went in and out among us for four months. One month, also, he was in America and one month in Holland, and in both countries labored unceasingly. For his ministry of the Word of Christ in the United Kingdom, thousands give thanks to God. By his established position as a writer, by his years, by his special gift from God, and by the power of the Holy Spirit, he was enabled to accomplish a service whose influence and result will long remain among us.

In a letter of farewell written on board ship, Mr. Murray thus took leave of the many friends he left behind:

LOVE—PRAYER—GOD

My beloved brothers and sisters,

May I in parting pass on these three words from our last day's meetings to you all? *Love* in the Spirit to each other, and to all saints; *prayer* in the name of Jesus; *God,* our Almighty God, to be waited on and trusted —this is a threefold cord that cannot be broken. In the faith that our God is visiting His people, and is very near to bless them with large increase of the spirit of love and prayer, and faith in their God, I commend you to Him.

I remain,

Andrew Murray

Contents

That They All

May Be One

That They All May Be One

I pray...That they all may be one;
as thou, Father, art in me,
and I in thee,
that they also may be one in us:
that the world may believe
that thou hast sent me.
And the glory which thou gavest me
I have given them;
that they may be one,
even as we are one.
I in them, and thou in me,
that they may be made perfect in one:
and that the world may know
that thou hast sent me,
and hast loved them,
as thou hast loved me.
—John 17:20-23

T he words from which I wish to speak to you are found in John 17. We shall take out of verse 20 the words, *"I pray."* Then in verse 21: *"That they all may be one; as Thou, Father, art in Me, and I in Thee, that they also may be one in Us: that the world may believe that Thou hast sent Me."* Verse 22: *"And the glory which Thou gavest Me I have given them."* Note that the twentieth verse says, *"I pray [or, I ask Thee]."* The twenty-second verse says, *"The glory which Thou gavest Me I have given them [with the same object]: that they may be one, even as We are One."* The twenty-third: *"I in them, and Thou in Me, that they may be made perfect in one; and that the world may know that Thou hast sent Me, and hast loved them, as Thou hast loved Me."*

If I judge correctly what fills your hearts this morning, then I think I would express it this way: there is a deep consciousness that there is not among the people of God that overflowing love that there should be. There is the desire to see this changed, and there is the secret faith: if God chooses, He is able to change us. But there is more. Your coming here is, I trust, a testimony to the positive expectation: if we ask Him, He will pour out more love among His people. We want this morning to make confession of this lack of love, we want to cry to God for an increase of love.

I need not remind you of what the proofs are that love is so often lacking. I will not speak of the divisions among the churches; I will not speak of the way in which Christians can speak of each other; I will not speak of the coldness often existing between Christians who spend years together in the same church, and eat the same bread at the Lord's Supper; I will not speak of how the most precious truths and promises of God unconsciously become walls of separation. You all know, you all deplore, that there is not that love whereby the world is compelled to say, "God has loved them, and has poured His love into their hearts."

And now, if we are to make confession, and if we are to be encouraged to pray and to hope and to expect deliverance, nothing is better than that we should turn for a few minutes to God's blessed Word—the words of our great High Priest in His last prayer. You know them well. He prayed: *"Father,...I pray that they all may be one."* It was God who was to do it. And then He added wonderful words to the effect: "Father, between You and Me there never has been anything but love, and I want that to be among My people, that they may be one, even as We are One."

And then He says, in other words: "Father, it will be such a wonderful thing!" When selfish, proud men learn to love as the Father and the Son of God love, the world will be compelled to say, "That is more than human love; that is a love that comes from heaven."

And then Christ said, in effect, "Father, it is for this that I have given them the glory that You gave Me, and have made them partakers of the Divine nature, and of all that You have. And, Father, on that account I pray for them. I have given them the glory You gave Me. And now, Father, watch over that glory, that they may be one as We are, and that they may be made perfect in one, that the world may believe that You have sent Me, and have loved them as You have loved Me." What a prayer!

Now, what are the thoughts that that prayer suggests to us about the oneness of God's people?

First, **the oneness among God's people is to be the reflection of the life of God in heaven.** Just think of that! Heaven is the place where the glory of God is perfectly manifested; earth is the place where the reflection of that glory is to be seen. Yonder in the heavens the sun burns in all its brightness and heat and glory; here on earth, miles and miles away, is the place where its light is shining. And yonder in heaven is the glory of God's love; but here on earth it is a beautiful, reflected light. And what is that light to be? We are to love one another and be one, just as the Father and the Son are One.

Oh, beloved, have we really taken it in? Think of the love of the Father to the Son. What is it? The Father gave all that He had to the Son. That is His love, and that is to be my love to you and your love to me. It is to be nothing less, for that is holiness, that is perfection, that is happiness. And God wants you holy and perfect and happy and like Himself. That is love. God gave all He had to His beloved Son.

And what was the love of the Son to the Father? He gave all back. When He had taken a human body, when He had come here in the flesh, He gave all. He gave His obedience, He gave His life, He gave all to the Father. That was love. He loved the Father in eternity and sought nothing for Himself. And He loved the Father amid temptation and amid His sufferings on the earth.

And now that love of the Father to the Son, and that love of the Son to the Father, is to be the measure of your love to each other, children of God. I do not ask, "Have you attained that?" But

I may ask, "Have you aimed at that? And has it been your study and heart's cry: 'Oh, God, help me to love as You love, and as Jesus loves'?"

Yes, the Lord Jesus said so in effect, distinctly, and more than once: *"A new commandment I give unto you, that ye love one another, as I have loved you"* (John 13:34). He came with that love, and He was prepared by the Holy Spirit to implant it in the hearts of the disciples, who had been unloving. *"Love one another, as I have loved you."* Christ gave us that command. Have we understood it? It is sometimes necessary to talk about the lack of love in the church of Christ, and it is sometimes necessary to forget it, and to come to my own heart and to ask, "How is it with my love to the brethren?"

That is our first thought: the oneness of God's people is to be the reflection of the very life of God in heaven.

Then next is: **that oneness is to be the manifestation of the mighty power of God.** It is a thing God has to do. The Lord Jesus Christ did not say, "Father, they are one." He said, *"I pray ...that they all may be one."* God was to do it. Just as Christ asked God to glorify Him in heaven in the beginning of the prayer, so here at the end He asked the Father in effect: "Do this, too, and grant that they may be one, even as We are." Beloved, God has to do it.

And there comes the great fault, there comes the great reason why there is so little love. We do not count upon God to do it. God puts into the heart of every child of His who is born of the Holy Spirit a seed, a principle, a power of Divine love, a new will, a new heart; and every child of God is by his very nature inclined to love God's children.

But after a time there comes trial, and it becomes difficult to love. And the Christian often begins to try in the power that is in him to love as he should, but he fails. Afterwards he gives way to despair, and he begins with his little love to do his very best, but he never can love as the Bible wants him to love. Ah! He misunderstood God's plan. God's plan is: *"It is God who worketh in you both to will and to do."* When He has first worked to will, you are still impotent, but He wants you to come and claim the power of the Holy Spirit to enable you to do.

I have spoken much and long about the Holy Spirit, but I am coming to the conviction, which I may say every day grows deeper, that we know very little of what the Holy Spirit can do. I believe that that word of St. Paul, *"The love of God shed abroad in our hearts by the Holy Ghost,"* means that just as Paul was filled with the love of God, and as Paul could say, *"The love of Christ constraineth me,"* and as Paul lived incessantly, day and night, praying for His people, and as Paul poured out his love with all the tenderness of a mother or a nurse as he tells us himself, so God's Holy Spirit can so fill the heart and life that love shall be to us as natural as the love of a mother towards her child. The Lord Jesus Christ, our High Priest, cried to His Father to do the work, to make us one. And we try in our own strength to love, and fail, instead of coming, utterly impotent and helpless, to claim a new blessing, to claim that the Holy Spirit shall fill us and shed abroad through our whole being the almighty love of God.

It is well we have come together today. My heart is glad to see God's children longing to hear about love. But everything will be like *"the morning cloud and the early dew."* Our aim and purpose to love will vanish unless God gives His Holy Ghost in power into our hearts. Do let every heart bow before God this morning. We are going to undertake the work of love, and give up ourselves to intercession, and think of what God wants us to do in intercession. But if we are really to have the spirit of intercession we must have the love of our Emmanuel, the Lamb of God. Come this morning and ask God to give you, in a measure and in a way and in a power you have never understood—and even now He can set your heart upon it—His almighty love. God can make your heart a vessel for that love, and He will delight to do it.

Then comes my next thought, and that is: **love comes in answer to prayer.** I have spoken about the great power of God doing it, but I now want to point out that Christ prayed for it.

He prayed: *"That they all may be one."*
Oh, that our hearts might just for a
moment look up to see our Lord Jesus
and hear by the Holy Spirit that prayer
which goes up, not in words, but in His
holy presence and power: *"Father,...that
they all may be one."* He prays for them
without ceasing, He lives to pray for
them.

And what does that call us to? To
praying with Him in His name, and in
His spirit, and with great faith in the
fellowship of His intercession. When we
pray far more for an outpouring of love
in our hearts and the hearts of God's
children around us, a change in the
Church will come.

Allow me here, my beloved friends,
to come at once to what has been on my
heart, and is on my heart—that God's
children ought every day of their lives
to pray for all believers. Paul did not
tell Christians in his epistles to pray for

the heathen, or for the Jews, or for the unconverted, but he always told them to pray for *"all saints."* They are the members of your body, they are your brothers and sisters. And until in our daily devotions we every day cry to God for His body the church, just as much as we cry to Him for our own souls, I do not believe that a great revival of love will come. But I think God will pour it into the hearts of His children as the beginning, as the earnest of what He is going to do. Do pray for Christians every day of your lives. I do not want you to give up any union that you may have joined, to pray at certain times for certain circles, or for all believers, but I want you to feel that it ought to be a continuous part of the spiritual life.

Just as close as is my relation to Christ is my relation to my fellow Christians; just as dependent as I am upon Christ in some things, I am dependent for others on the fellowship of the saints. Every thought of Christ ought to be linked with the thought of His people, His body the church. By prayer it will come. May God, before we part this morning, give us the very spirit of prayer to call upon Him. But may God give the spirit of prayer in our hearts in such a way that there shall be going up the cry from us continually: "Oh, God, make us one, as You and Your Son are One." The cry will lead us to feel our own impotence, and the loneliness and feebleness of our lives.

Remember that Paul said in I Thessalonians 4: 9-10: *"Ye yourselves are taught of God to love one another. And indeed ye do it."* And yet he wrote beseeching them, *"That ye increase more and more."* There is increase of love when the Holy Ghost touches the heart. Then the love will flow in a stream, and it will be one of those streams of which

Jesus spoke when He said: *"He that believeth in Me, out of him shall flow rivers of living water"* (John 7:38). Those living waters are to impart what the fountain has got, and thereby make all around green and fresh: the stream of love will impart of itself to bless others. We must pray that this oneness may be made manifest.

But another thought is this: **the manifestation of this oneness upon earth is to be a proof to the world that God sent Christ and that God has loved us.** Just think of that. How important it is! You know Christ Jesus Himself said: *"By this shall all men know that ye are My disciples [a heavenly people], if ye have love one to another"* (John 13:35). That is to be the heavenly hallmark, and He says it twice in our text.

First of all, He says, *"I pray that they may be one, that the world may* know that Thou hast sent Me." You know that Christ was among them in the world, and they would not believe it. And what was to bring conviction? Love. That is what Christ said. Not preaching, but love. Preaching is needed—praise God for what it does!—but love will do more.

In the next place He says: *"And the glory which Thou gavest Me I have given them; that they may be one, even as We are One; that the world may know that Thou hast sent Me, and hast loved them, as Thou hast loved Me."* God loved Christ with a wonderful love, and God loves His people with the same love; and the love with which God loves Christ became a love that He poured out upon us even unto the blood of Calvary. And the love with which God and Christ love us will be within us a power that will pour itself out, in the first place, for the brethren; and thereby the world will be convinced.

People speak of the evidences of Christianity, and books have been written on the evidences of Christianity, and they are not without their value, though I do not know that they have turned many from darkness to light. But Christ says it is love that will compel the world to say: "These men have got something from heaven. These men are living a superhuman life. Look at the way in which they love each other!" Dear friends, has the world around you, or any part of it, been convinced, been convicted, and been brought to acknowledge: "God sent Christ, and God loved you just as He loved Christ; I can see it, for there is something in you that I do not find upon earth?" Praise God!

There have been such cases. There are believers of whom others have felt

that they have something that is not of
the earth. But how little it is the case!
And why should it not be the case with
each one of us? It is just this: one thing
is needed. We must wait upon God in
prayer. Let me point out to you one text
to impress that thought upon you. In I
Thessalonians 3:12, what do we read?
*"And the Lord make you to increase and
abound in love one toward another."*
Now note that just as Christ prayed to
the Father, so Paul prayed: *"The Lord
make you to increase and abound in
love."* And he uses the same expression
in the ninth and tenth verses of the
fourth chapter: *"As touching brotherly
love ye need not that I write unto you;
for ye yourselves are taught of God to
love one another. And indeed ye do it
toward all the brethren which are in all
Macedonia; but we beseech you,
brethren, that ye increase more and
more."* Christ said in effect: *"Love one*

27

another, as I have loved you." And Paul said the same: *"The Lord make you to...abound in love, even as we do toward you."*

And now I press upon you to notice those words which follow in I Thessalonians 3: *"To the end He may establish your hearts unblamable in holiness before God."* Did ever you notice that *"to the end?"* How is God going to make me a holy man, and **to establish my heart** unblamable in holiness? By filling me with love. Love is the fulfilling of the whole law, and the perfection of the life of God and of Christ. And when God makes us to increase in love and abound in love toward one another, then self sinks away, and the love of God takes possession, and the love and the holiness of God can grow and prosper and rule within us. Let us take that prayer today: "The Lord make us to increase and abound in love one toward another, to the end He may establish our hearts unblamable in holiness before Him."

In conclusion, what is needed if, in answer to prayer, this love of God is to come and take possession of our souls? **The heart must be utterly and absolutely given up to God to love.** May God this day enable us to see how little there has been of the real heavenly love within us! May God enable us to make confession of it! How much self has limited our love to people that we agree with, and to people that we like, and to people who think just as we do! How much our love has been limited within our own circle, and how little it has gone out, like the love of Christ, as love to the unworthy, to those who differ from us, to those who do not love us!

Ah, brethren, have you made a study of it, to love every man whom you feel you would rather be separate from? Have you made it a study to pray: "Lord, here is one in whom my love can triumph, in whom Your love can triumph; I want to love him as a brother?" May God give us the spirit of humiliation, to confess how little we have of the Divine love.

Just when we try, at times, we have the proof of how the spirit of love has not yet triumphed within us. But, praise God the Father on whom Christ called, to whom Paul prayed, to whom we come to pray today—the Father in heaven—wants to give His Holy Spirit of love to us. We want, even before we make intercession for an outpouring of the Spirit of love upon the church, to begin by asking for an outpouring of the Spirit into our own hearts. We want to say: "Lord God, empty our hearts of self; we desire to confess and give up everything that is selfish; we desire to study and aim at this one thing—to live on earth towards every brother as God and Christ live together in heaven."

But you might say: "But God and Christ see in Each Other nothing but what is lovely. How can They do otherwise than love Each Other? But my brother tempts me so! There is so much in him that is hard and unlovable!" Ah, yes, it was for that the Son of God came to earth, to prove that the love of God in heaven could stand the trials of life—every enmity, every shame, every suffering—and live through it all. And it is your high privilege to have your heart filled with the heavenly love of Christ Jesus, and to carry it through life; and it is your high privilege to begin and prove that you love your brother. You might find it difficult to love the ungodly, and yet you sometimes tell me: "I find it easier to love the ungodly than to love my very brother." Oh, what a proof of your blindness! Praise God for love to the ungodly. But that brother of yours, redeemed with the blood of Christ, made a member of one body in one Spirit with you through Christ Jesus —what a thought that you cannot love that brother!

Oh, come today and let us confess our sin, our utter impotence, and then let us look up in faith and claim the mighty power of God's Spirit. Let us claim in faith the promise in Romans 5:5: *"The love of God is shed abroad in our hearts by the Holy Ghost, who is given unto us."*

Then, when we have truly yielded ourselves up to God, let us begin to plead and pray for God's church around us, for every professing child of God in London and in England. But let us begin to pray a prayer that shall never any day of our lives cease: "Lord, visit

Your saints." Oh, that God may write
this upon our hearts! Who are willing to
give themselves up to this glorious work
of praying for the saints of God and for
a revelation of God's love in Christ's
body? Let your hearts say to God: "Lord,
here am I." That will help you to get a
blessing of love for yourselves.

If you want love for yourselves, or
love which is going to plead for the body
of Christ, then you must do two things.
Go and confess to God your lack of love,
and then say: "Lord God, I want to have
that love, that from this day I may daily
pray for Your body, for all believers."
God will give it; the great intercession
of Christ secures it.

The Secret of

Effectual Prayer

The Secret of Effectual Prayer

Likewise the Spirit
also helpeth our infirmities:
for we know not what
we should pray for as we ought:
but the Spirit itself
maketh intercession for us
with groanings
which cannot be uttered.
And He that searcheth the hearts
knoweth what is the mind
of the Spirit,
because He maketh intercession
for the saints,
according to the will of God.
—Romans 8:26-27

I n these words we have the secret of effectual prayer. Since the morning meeting someone complained to me, "I feel so little love for prayer and power for prayer!" There is the power for prayer—the Holy Spirit. So many complain that they do not feel strong stirrings of desire in intercession for others. There is the secret power: *"the Spirit helpeth our infirmities."* Would God grant that we could learn that precious lesson!

What are the thoughts suggested to us here?

The first thought is this: **if you want to discover the secret of effectual prayer, you must begin with a sense of your own ignorance.** When does the Holy Spirit come? When a man says, "I cannot pray." But when a man says, "I can pray," there is not room for the Spirit to work in full power. Alas! How often we think it is easy to pray. We think, "I learned it from my mother; I learned it from my minister; I learned it when I was converted; I learned it from written prayers." And so, though we think we know how to pray, there may be at the back, alas, a deep ignorance of praying for what God wants us to pray for. We may be praying very earnestly for what we think, and yet not allowing God's Spirit to teach us what God thinks.

Therefore, if you want to pray in power begin with this word: *"The Spirit also helpeth [is given to help] our infirmities."* Just as Paul said, *"When I am weak then am I strong...that the power of Christ may rest upon me"* (II Corinthians 12:10, 9). So it is here. When I feel my infirmities in prayer, then the Holy Spirit will help me. It is when I learn to say—and not only to say, but when I live in the experience and consciousness—"I know not what I should pray for as I ought," that I have a claim upon the promise of the Holy Spirit's help.

Have you ever studied the blessedness of ignorance? Oh, the Divine blessedness of ignorance! *"God hath chosen the foolish things of the world"* (I Corinthians 1:27). That is no mere idea—it is a reality. Abraham went out not knowing where he went, and he had God for his Guide because he did not know where he was going. So through the whole of God's Word you will find it continually comes up that when a man is ignorant and at his wit's end and says: "I know not what to do," God comes in to take charge.

Remember the Holy Spirit cannot come to you in prayer as the Spirit of prayer and intercession unless this double thought is deep in your life: "I do not know rightly what to pray for, and I do not know how to pray as I ought."

There are so many Christians who think that that thought is a terrible burden and a great sorrow. But I tell you it is your highest privilege, if you use it aright, and say: "Lord, I cannot pray, but let Your blessed Spirit pray with me."

In this great work of intercession that we are going to be engaged in, and to talk about, and to undertake. Not only for today, but for the future, let us remember that our ignorance will be the secret of success if we use it correctly. "I know what to pray for," you say. "Yes, I can read my Bible. I know the needs of my heart. I know the needs of the world around me. Oh yes, I need to pray for London, and for God's church, and for the heathen." Oh, how much of that praying is the work of the mind, the work of the flesh, the work of man! Do not be afraid of letting that word take hold of you: *"We know not what to pray for as we ought."* That is the first step.

What is the next? **That we begin to learn that the Holy Ghost has been given from heaven into our hearts to teach us to pray.** *"The Spirit...helpeth our infirmities."* Have you realized that God not only answers prayer, but that God, dwelling within us by the Holy Ghost, inspires prayer? If that is true, what would be the effect of my believing fully?

It would be, first of all, an abasement before God, and a humiliation, and a dependence expressed thus: "Oh, God, may I not, in the power of the flesh, with the thought of my mind, hinder that blessed Spirit." And then there would come a deep subjection and surrender to the Spirit, and the deep consciousness: "I must give up my life for Him to live in me, or He cannot pray in me." We should then get rid of that terrible thought that we can at times get the Holy Spirit to come and do something for us. We should understand that He must be the very spirit of our lives, and He must have entire possession of us.

Have you ever learned this solemn, blessed lesson: the Holy Spirit and I are linked together in prayer? And God desires the Holy Spirit, dwelling in the body of Christ, should teach each individual of that body to pray aright in the power of faith. Have you ever learned that lesson? If not, may God open it up to you this afternoon.

And when the question comes, "What is needed that I may get the teaching of the Spirit?" the answer will be this: "As a surrendered soul, I am entirely at His disposal. He is not a person outside of me. He comes in to be my very life, and unless I give myself up to Him, how can He do His blessed work and fully teach me how to pray?"

That brings us to a very solemn point in this meeting. Some days ago, someone was telling me of another person that she wanted to bring with her, and she said, "I am afraid she is not a surrendered soul." In another case somebody said of one who was going to come, "Ah, that is one who is still undecided—half-way between Christ and the world!"

Now, if there are here souls, children of God, who are not utterly surrendered to Him, I plead with you, before I go further. By the mercy of God, think of it! The Holy Spirit cannot dwell in a worldly heart; the Holy Spirit cannot do His blessed work in a life that is not given up to Him. Come today, if you have any desire for a full blessing, and say: "If God has given His Holy Spirit to pray in me, I will give my whole heart to Him." If you have never yet in faith claimed the promise of the full indwelling of the Holy Ghost, come today and claim it. Your God offers you the Holy Spirit to pray in you, and how can He do it if you grieve Him, if you distrust Him, and if, by unbelief, you dishonor Him? Oh, I want to invite all God's children here to become intercessors. But we cannot do it unless we all join and say: "O God, reveal to us everything in which the Holy Ghost does not have complete possession. We desire to give it up, and to be filled with Your Spirit."

I feel more and more deeply, every time I address meetings, that you may have an earnest Christian, a godly man or woman, and yet his or her life is far below what God could make it, if he or she would only wait for the Holy Spirit to get possession. Believers, I want to call you to be intercessors. I want to plead with you by the needs of London with its five millions of people, by the needs of heathenism with its hundreds of millions, and by the needs of the church of Christ—alas! alas!—with its multitudes of nominal professors and half-hearted Christians, will you not be intercessors? Will you not give up yourselves to walk in the footsteps of Christ and to become fountains of blessing to this weary world? Oh, come and let the Holy Ghost have you entirely today, and then He will teach you how to pray.

A third thought is this: **we must understand the way in which the Holy Spirit will pray.** And what is that? *"The Spirit also helpeth our infirmities; for we know not what we should pray for as we ought; but the Spirit itself maketh intercession for us with groanings which cannot be uttered."* What is that? Prayers too deep for words! That is what we want. When the words can rise into prayer so fluently and so easily, alas, the depth of the heart is often not stirred. But what is it that the Holy Spirit wants to do? How often we see it in our blessed Lord Jesus? Do we not read that He once said: *"I have a baptism to be baptized with; and how am I straitened till it be accomplished!"* (Luke 12:50). You remember again that He said: *"And what shall I say? Father, save Me from this hour"* (John 12:27). He did not know at the moment what He should say. And yet again you know how in Gethsemane He wrestled and wrestled, and yet had but few words with which to utter the agony of His heart. Oh, brethren, when the Holy Spirit comes within us as the fire of God's love for souls, and we begin to think of the state of Christ's body, of our brethren in the church of Christ, of our own lack of love and tenderness and gentleness, of the feebleness that marks God's people, of the way the world loves to scorn our puny efforts, and of the millions that are going down to misery—surely there will come to us, if God's Spirit only had possession of us, a burden and a sorrow and an intensity and desire too deep for words! Then is the time when the Holy Spirit prays in us *"with groanings which cannot be uttered."*

We read of creation *"groaning."* There is a moan throughout creation, and a longing for redemption. The animals do not speak it out in words, but throughout creation there is a groan. Even so, the deeper God's child is led into the fellowship of Christ and love for souls, the deeper and the truer his sympathy is with the perishing. Then there will come times when he can only sit still before God, and say: "Lord, what is to come of it? Oh, teach me what I may ask, teach me what I may pray." And while he feels, "I cannot pray," God has heard in that heart a better prayer than one that has flowed so smoothly and quickly from the lips.

Many think that when they have been in their closet and prayer has flowed easily, they have prayed well. And they think at other times, when prayer has not flowed easily, that they have not prayed well. And yet, if that silent prayer were mingled with true faith and waiting upon God, and a deep burning desire, it was a sweeter incense to the Father than a prayer that came in words. Oh, it is a solemn thing for the worm of the dust to get linked to the Holy Spirit of God. You cannot wonder that the Holy Spirit of God will sometimes come with wrestlings and groanings which cannot be uttered; but the privilege and blessedness are unspeakable. Oh, let us yield ourselves to Him.

And then comes the last thought in my text: **the believer must know how the answer will come.** How can it come when I sit there saddened and burdened with a burden I cannot speak out?

Listen! *"He that searcheth the hearts knoweth what is the mind of the Spirit, because He maketh intercession for the saints, according to the will of God."* Oh, think of that! God, the heart-searcher, is needed to find out the meaning of prayer. You think you know it, but you do not know it. It needs God in heaven, who searches the hearts, to measure the real value of a prayer. We deceive ourselves. We have sometimes felt: "Oh, that man can pray!" And we have thought he is a Christian, but we have been disappointed afterwards, for his life was not like his prayer. We have sometimes heard ourselves pray, and we have thought that God had helped, and yet afterwards we felt that that prayer showed only half the life. There was another half. But, ah! The Searcher of hearts never makes a mistake; the Searcher of hearts searches the Divine life of every breath of the Spirit.

Child of God, give yourself up to the Holy Spirit to pray even when you feel you can say little, and He that searches the hearts knows what the mind of the Spirit is. And why? It says, *"Because He maketh intercession for the saints."* Note the words *"for the saints."* I quoted this morning the words of Paul, *"With all supplication for all saints"* (Ephesians 6:18). Some think that the word does not only refer to those who are praying, but that it has a wider meaning, that it is the Holy Spirit's one work to make supplication for all saints. Therefore, if you want this power of the Holy Spirit to pray, you must not confine Him to one saint—to yourself merely—or you will lose a great deal. But you must take Him for what He is given for—to make supplication and intercession for all saints. Unite yourself to Him, and let Him unite Himself to you, and give up yourself to make intercession for all saints.

The Holy Spirit prays within us, and God searches the hearts. There is nothing that God delights to find so much as love in and for all of His children. I do pray you to make a study of that. Suppose you hear of a legalist. The inclination is to condemn him. You stand at the very opposite pole and think how he may be destroying the religious life of some. But, oh, do remember to pray for him! You may hear a man—a child of God—speak, and you think, "He is not in my view sound in doctrine," and you have a sharp word about him. But, I beseech you, pray for him. If there be one in your circle who has grieved you, love and pray for him. Make intercession.

Need I remind you that the thought is a very wonderful one? Christ sits as a king upon the throne. Yes, and what is the work of a king? To rule, to have honor and power and glory and dominion. And Christ has that. But with all that, upon His kingly throne He ever lives to pray. If some king on earth spent all his free time in praying for his subjects, how the sound would go abroad of the piety and godliness of that man! But, oh, our King's great work is to pray, and His great object in sending down the Holy Ghost into our hearts is that we should pray with Him.

Christians, how much of your life have you given up to intercession? Or how little? God knows. There is not one in this hall who has not reason to blush at the fact. God forgive us! And God work a change by His almighty grace. And God strengthen every one who is trying to learn to pray. Someone in a note expressed a hope that this would be "a day with Christ in the school of prayer." God grant it! Oh, that our great Intercessor and High Priest might condescend to breathe upon us, and to touch us, and to draw us, and to link us with Himself in prayer! But He can only do it as our hearts are given up to the Holy Ghost.

Let me conclude by pointing out what the work is that we have this afternoon. We want to intercede for London very definitely. May God bless every prayer circle that binds His children together to cry to Him. But we need something more. Oh, that without any prayer union, and without any organization, all God's children could learn: "I am anointed of the Holy Ghost, the Spirit of intercession, that I may do my work!"

What is the reason of the feeble Christianity that there is in the world? What is the reason that there are so many souls here complaining of the lack of power and joy? It is this—the selfishness of our religion. We have come to Christ to be saved, and that is the chief thing. And then a little intercession and a little work we do alongside with the rest.

But we must come round to an entirely different position. We must say: "I have been redeemed to be a member of Christ's body, and, like Christ, to live holy and be a blessing to the world, and like Christ, to communicate God's love to my fellow men."

But you cannot do that without giving up yourselves entirely to Him. God be praised for every child of His whose eyes have been opened to see it, and whose heart has been stirred to make the blessed choice: "Yes, Lord, everything, every breath, that Your name may be exalted!" God be praised for every child of His in whose heart this afternoon is the consciousness: "That has not been my life, but I am going to live it." God help us!

But we not only want to pray for London; we want to take a little time for further intercession and to plead especially for God's children. I cannot press upon you too earnestly to pray for all saints. In the interval it was suggested that we should have an All Saints Prayer Union. We do not want a new organization, by any means, but it may be that God will lead us in that direction, and you may hear about it later. But I charge you to take it up as your life's work to bear the state of the Christian church before God in heaven. Live to pray. You pray for your work, and for your circle, and for many interests, and I praise God for it. Pray for these, and not less. But pray first and pray most, in the power of the Spirit of intercession, for all saints. Pray for every believer in the world, and that will fill your heart with love.

Pray for every believer whom you know to be wrong, or to be doing something wrong, or whom you think to be doing something wrong—and you cannot long pray for a man without beginning to love him and to be humbled before the Lord. May God pour out His Spirit. May God teach us what it means that the Holy Spirit is the Spirit of intercession!

Oh, beloved, you have heard more than one address and appeal from time to time for many years about the baptism of the Holy Spirit, or you have read them. You have heard appeals about being filled with the Spirit, about being led by the Spirit, about walking in the Spirit. But remember, the Spirit is the Spirit of intercession for all saints. You cannot have Him to yourself. He is the Spirit of the body.

Today let us do two things. On the one side, let us give up ourselves to the Holy Spirit as the Spirit of intercession to pray in us, and let us say that we desire to live for God, and for His church. On the other side, in our prayers continually and in our life, let this thought be our joy and our strength: "However ignorant I feel, and however feeble my words have been, the Spirit prays in me, and God who searches the hearts knows the mind of the Spirit."

With Eagles'

Wings

With Eagles'
Wings

They that wait upon the Lord
shall renew their strength;
they shall mount up
with wings as eagles;
they shall run, and not be weary;
and they shall walk, and not faint.
—Isaiah 40:31

The subject announced for this evening was *Working and Waiting.* All that we have been asking God to do must manifest itself in new work, and more work, and better work. Those who have never worked cannot have been in earnest this morning in asking God to honor them with the indwelling of His heavenly love, if they are going to live selfish lives. They cannot have been honest when they prayed the prayer: "Oh, God, let Your own blessed love fill me, and then I will spend it. I will give it out. I will scatter the blessing." And those who have been working, oh, how conscious they are of the feebleness of their work! It is not always more work that is needed—some might with advantage work less. The main thing is the quality of work that is done.

This afternoon we prayed God for His mercy upon London, and upon the workers in London, and for grace that everyone of us might go out to live in the power of God's strength and God's love. It is hardly necessary that I should speak much to you about the secret of strength for work. That is what we all need. There is promised and prepared for us, as God's children, a Divine strength. But how many are unconscious of it! They know not the way to receive it. And just as that one word *work* means so much, earthward and manward, so that word *wait* means everything Godward. And your work towards men, if it is to bring blessing, will depend entirely upon your waiting upon God.

Listen to the words of my text: *"They that wait upon the Lord shall renew their strength."* Every day, *"they shall run, and"* never *"be weary; they shall walk, and not faint."* Blessed life! To work, work, work, sometimes in weariness of body and of mind, sometimes in despair and failure, and yet never to be weary in spirit, and always to be carried on in the joy of God! What a kind Master! You can see in His servants that He cares for them. His servants are children and heirs of God, and will God allow them to be weary in spirit? Never, if they will come and dwell with Him as He is ready to have them. They that wait upon the Lord shall renew their faith, and shall always be strong for work.

Oh, that I had known that when I was a young minister! Oh, that I knew it fully even tonight! I thank Him for what He has shown me of it. But, oh, that He might reveal fully to my soul and to every soul here that they who wait upon the Lord, their strength shall be always new; *they shall run, and not be weary; they shall walk, and not faint!* How many are faint-hearted in their work, and stop working, or work wearily, or work very little, or work with effort and struggle? And all because they do not know the joy of the Lord! May God teach us tonight how to work.

They that wait upon the Lord shall renew their strength; they shall mount up with wings as eagles." Let me take that one expression first. Most of you have heard sermons preached on that text, I am sure, or read expositions of it. But just let me give you two or three very simple thoughts about the mounting up on eagle wings.

You know the eagle is called the king of birds, and it is said to fly the highest of all birds, and to go straight toward the sun. And this king of birds is taken to be the image of God's children. Why? What are eagles' wings for? To carry the king of birds high up into heaven.

And, Christian, you are a heavenly man, and you are to lead a heavenly life. Your place is in the heavenlies. And how can you rise to heaven unless you have eagle wings to mount with? But, thank God if He created the eagles with their wings to rise high heavenward, He can give me eagle wings, so that I too can rise upward. Yes, the believer is to live a heavenly life. His home is within the veil, in the holiest of all. He is to walk on *"high places."* He is to live in the love of God unclouded; he is to live with the joy of heaven in his heart; he is to live a life in which the will of God is done, as in heaven so on earth. The Christian needs eagle wings.

But, alas! How many Christians are bound and weighed down here below! Once when I was in Switzerland I saw an eagle, a splendid bird, but it was chained to a rock. It had some twenty or thirty feet of chain attached to its legs and to an iron bolt in the rock. There was the king of birds, meant to soar into heaven, chained down to earth.

That is a picture of multitudes of believers. Is that your life? Are you just dragging along through the Christian life? You are a child of God. That eagle was a king of birds, a noble king, but something kept it down. Are you allowing business, are you allowing the cares of the world, are you allowing the flesh, to chain you down, so that you cannot rise up? God forbid it should be so. I invite every believer to say tonight: "God help me to mount up on eagle wings; I want to live the heavenly life." God help us!

And then you ask me, "How can I get these eagle wings?"

I answer, "How did the eagle get its wings? By its birth. It was born a royal eagle; it had a royal descent."

And every child of God is born with eagle wings. But, alas! They know it not. And, alas! It is not sufficiently preached. And, alas! The realization of it is not sufficiently sought from God. We are all born with eagle wings; we have within us a Divine nature; we have within us the very Spirit of Christ Jesus to draw us heavenward. But how many believers there are who do not know that they have the Spirit of heaven within them, and how many there are who just barely know it, but do not think of it, and accept it, and rejoice in it! And how many there are who have got a little inkling of it, but are unfaithful, and turn themselves away toward the world again! Oh, Christians, I tell every one of you tonight, you have a Divine nature, you have a heavenly nature; God means you to live a heavenly life.

You tell me, "If I have these eagle wings I have never learned to use them. How can I learn to use them?"

I will give you the answer. You have heard it before perhaps, but listen once again. In Deuteronomy Moses tells us about God, how, just as the eagle soars up to its nest and flutters over its young and carries them on its back, so God carried Israel. What does that mean?

Look at the distant precipice of cliffs at the side of the sea, some thousand feet high, and up on a ledge of rock there is an eagle's nest, and the little birds have just been hatched out. Come another day, and what do you see? The nest is nothing but a number of sticks gathered together and laid across, and there are the little eaglets. The mother eagle comes, stirs up her nest with her beak and claw, and scatters it. And then what does she do? The little eaglets have looked over the cliff, and they have seen the deep sea down below, and they are afraid. The mother, however, casts them over, and then they go fluttering about and threatening to fall and be drowned. But see how she hangs over them, and goes in under them, and stretches her broad wings, and catches first the one and then the other, and carries them on her back to some place of safety. God made the eagle with that instinct, and that is nothing but a picture of God's own heart.

How does God teach His eaglet children to use their wings? He comes and stirs up their nests. How does He do that? Sometimes with a trying providence, with a death, with sickness, with loss, with some tribulation, with temptation. And why? Just as those eaglets, ready to sink, find the mother coming under them and carrying them, so the everlasting arms are stretched out underneath **the soul that feels itself** ready to perish, and God calls upon the soul to trust Him. As the eaglet trusts the mother to carry it, my God asks me to trust Him, that He will bear me. The mother bears the little eaglet time after time, and it begins to take courage, and at last is ready to soar forth, for it has learned to use its wings. The mother taught it. And my

God longs to teach His children to mount on eagle wings.

But how can they do it? It says: *"They that wait upon the Lord shall mount up with wings as eagles."* Yes, God often comes to the Christian worker and stirs up the nest, because He sees the eagle wings are not being used. God finds a worker very earnest, and perhaps for a time there has been blessing, but somehow self-will and the power of the flesh have come in. He has trusted in himself, and God comes and stirs up the nest. Then the question comes to the Christian worker: "What is this? Have I served my God as I might have done, or have I sinned against Him?"

Then His blessed Word comes with a message to this effect: "No, your Father loves you, but there is one thing He misses about you—you are not heavenly enough. You have worked hard, and you have worked well, and you have worked successfully; but the tenderness and the beauty of the heavenly love of Jesus are too little seen in you. The Father wants you to mount up on eagle wings. Your fellowship with God is not as tender as it ought to be, so God has stirred and broken up your nest." And then the worker is all dark and anxious, and fears that everything will perish. He finds not the power he once had. Praise God, if you just learn to see that God wants you to trust Him more, to come into closer union with Himself.

Beloved Christian, listen to God's Word: *"They that wait upon the Lord shall renew their strength."* They shall go on from strength to strength, they shall get stronger month by month, and year by year. They shall renew their strength, and they shall mount up with eagle wings. God, help us to believe it and to say tonight, "That is going to be my lot, a life of mounting up on eagle wings." Dare everyone say that? Yes, you dare say it, if you dare say, "My life shall be one of waiting upon God."

What is the characteristic of the eagle wings? To be able to mount up to heaven, the wings of the eagle must have greater strength than the wings of any other bird. And God wants His children to be so strong that they can live above the world and that they can show the men of the world: "I am living in another world." The great mark of the disciple of Christ that Christ spoke of in His prayer to the Father was: *"They are not of the world, as I am not of the world."* They belong to heaven, their life and heart are there. Oh, Christian, do believe that in your business in this city of London, in a house full of care and anxiety, as men speak, you can live a heavenly life in the peace and the love and the joy of God. Eagles' wings are strong wings; they can resist the gravitation and the attraction of earth, they can rise heavenward. Praise God, we can live heavenly lives!

Just look how this idea or strength is the great idea of our text, and how you have it in the words that precede in Isaiah 40:28-29: *"Hast thou not known? hast thou not heard, that the everlasting God, the Lord, the Creator of the ends of the earth, fainteth not, neither is weary? There is no searching of His understanding. He giveth power to the faint; and to them that have no might He increaseth strength."*

Let me ask you, weary worker, have you heard it, have you known it, that the everlasting God never is weary? You tell me, "Of course, I have known it all my life, and I have believed it." Then believe it in the application God makes.

You ask, "What is that application?" The application is, that if the everlasting God is never weary, you need never be weary, because your God is your strength. That is what the Bible teaches. You have no strength but what God gives, and you can have all the strength that God can give.

Have you heard it, weary worker? Have you heard it, Christian who fears that you can work but little? Have you heard it, earnest intercessor, who fears that the blessing will not come as you would have it? Listen! *"Hast thou not heard that the everlasting God, the Lord, the Creator of the ends of the earth, fainteth not, neither is weary?"* Oh, think of that!

You find that word *faint* four times in the passage. First, it is God *fainteth not;* then it is, He gives power to the *faint;* and then it is, the young men shall *faint.* All human strength shall faint; the very strongest shall faint and be of no avail. And last, *"They shall run, and not be weary; and they shall walk, and not faint."*

I pray you, understand this wonderful teaching. There is the Everlasting and Almighty One, and you are asked to look at Him with His mighty creative power, and His power in providence. This evening I read the verse: *"Lift up your eyes on high, and behold Who hath created those things: He calleth them all by names, by the greatness of His might, for that He is strong in power; not one faileth"* (Isaiah 40:26). Every star is made to preach to you that God cares for them all, and God's power upholds them. And God's power upholds you much more, child of God. Oh, that we might begin to believe tonight in the power of almighty God! I pray to God that I believe in it fully; my heart longs to do so.

I find that if there is one lesson we need to learn, it is the lesson of our impotence. When I was studying and learning to be a Christian as a young man, I was told a great deal about my lack of righteousness, and about my want of goodness, and about my absolute worthlessness. I believed it, and I believe it still. I have no righteousness before God in myself. But I was never taught aright. (At least I was not taught it so clearly as that it entered my heart. It may have been my fault, but since that time I have found so many who have not been taught it. I do not think I was ever taught correctly.) I was never taught that just as little righteousness as you have, just as little strength have you, and just as much as you are dependent on the righteousness of Christ alone for salvation, just so you are dependent on the strength of God alone for sanctification.

I was not taught that, and that is the truth of God. If you are to live holy lives and work for God, you must learn: "My only hope of being holy and working aright is the everlasting God in heaven."

Then follows the promise: *"He giveth power to the faint, and to them that have no might He increaseth strength."* God offers Himself to be the power and the strength and the might of every one of His children. Oh, is not that what we stand in need of in all our religious work—to get to that secret place of God's power, where the power of God can work in us?

You ask, and you cannot ask a more important question: "How can I get that power?" Listen to the glorious answer: *"They that wait upon the Lord shall renew their strength; they shall mount up with wings as eagles."* Where do I get the power to use eagle wings to mount and soar and rise higher and higher? In waiting upon God.

There are people who cannot understand that. One beloved brother in the ministry asked me last week, in connection with our meetings: "Is there not a danger of too great a passivity?"

I said: "Oh, yes, my brother, as long as we think it is our activity that must do it, then passivity robs us of time and strength. But once we understand that it is God that must work it in us, then I understand that my highest passivity will be my highest activity, for when I give myself entirely away to God, God can work in me. Then I shall work as one that waits upon the Lord."

Let us now for a few minutes try and think what this waiting on the Lord is. I want to give it you as my parting word. When I came to Exeter Hall six months ago, we had a breakfast, attended by a company of some one hundred and twenty friends. I spoke on that occasion, and gave one of the simplest messages that there could be to point out that waiting upon God is the one thing the church needs. I have been perfectly surprised to find what a response that simple word has created in the hearts of God's children. And so I give you that word tonight: *"They that wait upon the Lord shall renew their strength."*

What is needed to live such a life? My answer is, first of all, if you are to wait aright upon the Lord, you must learn to know Him. You must turn away your thoughts and eyes and heart and trust from everything, and set them upon God alone. My conduct in waiting for a man, or waiting on him, will depend entirely on what I think of him. One who waits upon the Queen behaves in a different way from one who waits upon an ordinary person. And all our waiting upon God will depend upon one thing—the knowledge that we have of Him.

But listen again. How does God reveal Himself when He calls upon us to wait upon Him? You have heard the words that I have read to point us to Himself as the Almighty Creator, and they tell us that just as His omnipotence created the world and is a guarantee for its maintenance, so the omnipotence of God is a guarantee for the strength of our Christian lives. Oh, take time to take it in. The Almighty God is with me to work in my heart all that He wants me to have. Is that true? Is God's omnipotence ready to work in me all that He expects of me? There is not a doubt about it, because I cannot work it. And He does not ask it of me except as He offers to work it.

Let me look at the omnipotence of God, and then at His faithfulness. He never is weary. He has kept the world going all these ages. And my short life of sixty, seventy, or eighty years—will my God not care for and maintain that? When I look at what He does for the stars, I realize that His work is done every moment. If He withdrew His hand one moment, the stars would fall. And God, in His omnipotence and faithfulness, is willing to work in my heart every moment of the day.

Moment by moment
I'm kept in His love,
Moment by moment
I've life from above,
Looking to Jesus
till glory doth shine,
Moment by moment,
Oh, Lord, I am Thine.

Do I keep my property, say my watch, moment by moment? And must you think, Christian, that your God will not keep you every moment? He will, if you will let Him. You are invited by Him to come, and day by day to make it the chief exercise of your religious life to wait upon what your God is going to do for you, to expect it of Him, to look to Him in confidence, and in the blessed assurance that He will do it all.

Are there here tonight any earnest Christians whose lives are not yet in the bright light of God's countenance? Let me speak a single word again to you about the blessedness of moment by moment living in Christ. This very afternoon I had a young lady here who wrote me a letter last week, and I will tell you the story she told me in her letter, which she confirmed this afternoon. At the meetings in Whitechapel, on the evening when we spoke about absolute surrender, she wrote me how word by word she approved, and understood, and accepted, until it came to the last, when the question was asked, "Will you now absolutely surrender?" Then her fears got the better of her, and she went away very miserable. She came again next morning and afternoon and evening, and then we spoke about the omnipotence of God *"The things that are impossible with men are possible with God"* (Luke 18:27). She fixed her eye upon Jesus, and she thought: "If that is true, Christ will strengthen me." And she had the power at once to make a joyful surrender. She wrote me how, three days later, she was able to prove that surrender in an act of obedience to God's voice.

Are there any of you who have not yet found the secret of a life in the full joy of Jesus' countenance and love all the day? Come tonight and claim Omnipotence to work it in you. Let the exchange be clear. God has given you all things in Christ, all spiritual blessings, all strength, all wisdom, everything in Him. You have been holding back; you have been afraid. You have perhaps been ignorant and never understood it, but come tonight and say: "Absolute surrender! Lord Jesus, You shall have everything." And trust in Him, trust in His omnipotence to work in you all that your God would have. *"They that wait upon the Lord shall renew their strength."* Count upon it that as you go out tonight and tomorrow, not to hold fearfully to what you have got, not by effort to maintain something that was given you, but in childlike abandonment and simple faith to say, "I am counting upon God to work it all in me." Take that word tonight. That is the life of strength and of joy: *"They that wait upon the Lord shall renew their strength."*

But again, I have said that the first great thing we need in order to live a life of waiting upon God is to know the God upon whom we wait: study God, study to know Him. But the second is to know ourselves—to be willing and determined to accept what God reveals about us. And what does God reveal in contrast with His great omnipotence? Our utter impotence. I said a little while ago that many people believe they have no righteousness, but they do not believe they have no strength. But accept that word tonight: *"He giveth power to the faint; and to them that have no might He increaseth strength"* (Isaiah 40:29). What a contrast! To a man with no might, no power, God increases strength; but if a man has a little power, God does not do it.

Do you not see that the great secret of waiting upon God is to be brought down to utter impotence? *"I can do nothing"* (I cannot too often repeat these words of the blessed Son of God) *"of Myself"* (John 8:28). What a mystery! Jesus said that, and He just waited upon God. And I ask you, child of God, would not you like to occupy the very place that Jesus did before the Father, and in the Father's heart? Would not you be willing to take that place, and to love every day as a man that has no might, but is utterly helpless, and just to wait upon God.

Oh, the deception is we think that we have so much strength and do not need to wait upon God. If a number of ships of war were sent out to sea, and were ready to start at any moment, and if the question "What are they waiting for?" were asked, the answer would likely be one of two things: either they were waiting for supplies, or waiting for orders. Perhaps the stores had not all been brought, and they were waiting for supplies; or else they were waiting for orders as to what was to be done.

Child of God, that is to be your position. First of all, you are to wait for supplies. Wait for the power of the Holy Spirit every day; wait for the strength of God every hour. Cultivate the habit of waiting on the Lord, and your supplies will come.

And also cultivate the habit of waiting for orders. Wait for instruction. God is willing to teach and guide His people in a way beyond their conception. Wait for instruction. Do not think, "I have my instructions in the Bible." You often mistake them and misapply them. Study and love your Bible, but remember it is God who must give the orders, and you will fail if you take them from a book. Love your Bible and fill your heart with it, but let God apply it in your daily life.

Once more, if I am to wait upon the Lord aright I must not only know my God and know myself, but I must study well what this word *wait* in itself implies.

It implies, first of all, patience. The Bible speaks about waiting patiently and also about waiting quietly. You must cultivate that habit. How can you do it? My answer is a very simple one. I might speak it to a child or a young Christian, and yet I find many older Christians who need it.

I will put it this way. When you go into your closet for your morning devotions, do not, as is very often done, read the Bible and think about it and pray about it, and then get up and go. But do something else in between. Before you read, set yourself still so that your soul may realize: "I am waiting for God to come in and take possession of me for today." That is your great need.

How many a child of God spends half an hour in his private room, in his quiet home, and he can tell you about so many beautiful thoughts in the chapter he read and what he prayed! But he has never got to this: that he knows, "My God is going to keep me all the day." And that is what you want to get in your morning prayer, an assurance from God that He will keep you. Then you will go out into your business in the world with His strong arm about you. Cultivate that habit before you read, and in the middle of your reading sometimes shut your eyes, and just sit quiet and say: "My God, in the midst of my reading, I wait on You to make the Word living in my heart." And then, before you pray, sit still, and shut your eyes, and say: "Will God now listen to me for certain? Shall I get an answer when I pray?" Get waiting upon God, and then kneel down and pray your prayer, very shortly, perhaps, and say, "Am I waiting upon my God?" Then pray very definitely what you want. Let your soul grow into the blessed consciousness, not that I have fed on some beautiful words of God, not that I have prayed this prayer very earnestly for this and that, but let your soul go out in your quiet hour in this one consciousness: "I have been waiting upon God, and God has answered me, and God will keep me today." Oh, learn to come into blessed fellowship with God, and never, never may you pray a prayer without the blessed thought: "As the eyes of servants look unto the hand of their masters, so our eyes wait upon the Lord our God." Wait quietly, wait patiently.

And then wait continually—not one or two hours, not one moment, but all the day. Take that text in Psalm 25:5, *"On Thee do I wait all the day."* Pray for the Holy Spirit to bring you into that blessed habit of waiting all the day upon God, to give you instruction, to guide, to order, to help, to give supplies of grace and joy and strength; and God will do it. *"Blessed are all they that wait for Him"* (Isaiah 30:18).

Our time will not allow us to speak longer, but just one more text: *"Men have not heard, neither hath the eye seen, what He hath prepared for him that waiteth for Him"* (Isaiah 64:4). Oh, learn to look to God for unexpected things. Learn to give up your thoughts about what God can do. Rest upon His promises to you, and plead them. Then you will find that God can do beyond what you can conceive. Expect God by the Holy Spirit to work in you something utterly beyond your comprehension, and God will do it—secretly, hiddenly, perhaps, without your feeling it, but God will do it if you trust Him for it. *"They that wait upon the Lord shall renew their strength."*

And now, before we part, we want to spend half an hour in waiting upon God together, and we want to plead with God, to make us all very strong in the strength of the Lord, and to give us all eagle wings. He has given them to us, and if we wait upon Him He will give us the grace to use them, to mount up, *"and to run, and not be weary; and to walk, and not faint."* God grant to us the spirit of waiting upon Him, for Jesus' sake. Amen.